Negotiating the Shadows

Negotiating the Shadows

Daily Meditations for Lent

RACHAEL A. KEEFE

WIPF & STOCK · Eugene, Oregon

NEGOTIATING THE SHADOWS
Daily Meditations for Lent

Wipf & Stock
An Imprint of Wipf and Stock Publishers
199 W. 8th Ave., Suite 3
Eugene, OR 97401
www.wipfandstock.com

ISBN 13: 978-1-60899-854-8

Manufactured in the U.S.A.

For Erika whose light leads me out of the shadows.

Contents

Preface

When you pass through the waters, I will be with you; and through the rivers, they shall not overwhelm you; when you walk through fire you shall not be burned, and the flame shall not consume you. For I am the Lord your God, the Holy One of Israel, your Savior. I give Egypt as your ransom, Ethiopia and Seba in exchange for you.

—ISAIAH 43:1–3

ASH WEDNESDAY ENCOUNTER

In my hands I hold a bowl of hope
oil and ash for anointing
a mark of dust,
of sins committed in thought, word, and deed

this is not why they come
not one needs to remember the dust
they come seeking the breath
Your breath
light in the darkness

they line up before me
brows wrinkled with worry
fear, pain, loss
bowed down with the burdens of living

they look to me for forgiveness
a simple mark of the cross
to give them hope in the face of their despair
it's not for me that they come,
it's You

will You not honor us with Your presence?
grace them with a whisper?
even echoes would be enough

they come seeking, hoping, wanting, needing
You went to the wilderness once
in the same manner
fasting, praying, seeking
with echoes of "Beloved" in Your ears
naming You,
claiming You

You went to find Yourself
we wander in the wilderness of our own making
more often than not
we lack the surety You found there

where You resisted the Tempter
we give in
we think that we can feed—or starve—
our hunger into submission
we think we can be strong by taking from others
or by losing ourselves
we think we can create our own gods

in Your wilderness wanderings
You found Yourself
and Your God
You stepped into the role of Beloved

so they step forward
asking for a sign of You
from You

I hold hope in my hands
their eyes hold doubt
and need
I give them what I can
a reminder that they do not walk alone
in the desert
in the dust
in their sin

it's hard for me to hold
this bowl of oil and ash
the promise of forgiveness
tumbles from my lips
but fails to reach my heart
or their eyes

who am I to lead this wilderness wandering?
I, too, listen for the echoes
but I hear silence
and yet this is why You went to the desert
for the silence and space
to confront and claim Yourself
to reach into brokenness and
draw out life

will You not draw life here
in this line of lost,
seeking, searching, doubting, sinning?

honor us with Your presence
bathe us in Your silence
until we can claim ourselves
until Beloved fills our ears
and the Tempter holds no power

their need fills the bowl
in exchange for
a simple cross of ash to adorn them
mark them Yours
will You not claim them
sit with them in their brokenness
until the possibility of healing
enters in?

my words are lost in the wilderness
absorbed by the heat and dust of the desert
but even whispers of You
would make a difference

they will go home
I am alone with a bowl too heavy to carry
there is no one who will put Your mark on me
if I am to lead
will You not guide?
in silence
I leave the bowl for You
and sit waiting, wanting, needing

forgiveness
wholeness
an echo of Beloved

will You not meet us in the wilderness?
we come seeking, praying, fasting
as You did once

claim us
as once You claimed Yourself

Beloved.

Acknowledgments

I N ACKNOWLEDGING all the people who encouraged, in-spired, or otherwise supported me in writing this book, I must begin with Merle Jordan. I would not have written this book if he hadn't insisted that I could. Words do not begin to express my gratitude. I am also indebted to my early readers who all encouraged me to keep writing: C. Elaine Watkins, John McGuirk, Tim Thomas, Derek VanGulden, Michael Livingston, John Hall and Erika Sanborne—you all made it much easier to finish this project. I also offer a special word of gratitude to my early listeners: Promise Church members, Star Island Mid-Week 1 '08, the women of South Church, and the New Hampshire Hospital com-munity—your enthusiasm and appreciation kept me go-ing. In addition, thank you to Beth Nordbeck, Mary Luti, Sharon Thornton, and Jed Rardin for your encouragement and support in getting this project written.

Introduction

S o many of us struggle to make meaning out of our lives or our world and often despair of finding hope or purpose for the days to come. I do not claim to have any answers. I offer my perspective after years of grappling with darkness to arrive at a place of acceptance of my value as a human being and a beloved child of God. My hope is that you will find comfort and challenge in my words, that you will experience Bible passages differently, and that you will be moved along in your Lenten journey to a place of new life.

Lent is a difficult season and most of us don't know quite what to make of it. At worst it is a forty-day diet plan. At best, it is a season of penitential reflection that gives way to new life. Churches have long-standing practices around Lent—worship, Bible study, chowder suppers, luncheons, Passion plays, and numerous other activities, spiritual and not. What seems less apparent are personal practices that challenge intellect and spirit. If Lent is a spiritual journey, then the road should be treacherous and the light of Easter not always visible. We ought to arrive at Good Friday warn out from wrestling our own demons and ready to offer up all the things which hold us captive to make room for the new life of Easter morning.

I offer the meditations in this book as potential guides along the way. I've used elements of my own struggles to know myself and my God and the stories others have shared with me to engage biblical texts in a new and relevant way.

Mostly, I've raised the questions of my spiritual journey and written them out here in hopes that you will hear echoes of your own searching and seeking. I don't avoid the dark, shadowy places of my life, our world, or my experience with church not to criticize or to dwell in difficulty but to lift them up to the light of hope.

Now that you know why I chose to focus on Lent, you might be curious about why I chose poetry for form. The answer is simple: poetry was my first love. I received a book of T.S. Elliot poems around age eight and have been hooked ever since. For me, poetry is verbal iconography. With poetry I can create inviting images and evoke deep emotions that might awaken something within you as you read or listen. And if I open the right window, point effectively toward Truth as I understand it, you might find a little light in your own darkness.

If you've picked up this book, you are likely searching for something. May you find it in the following pages. There is no wrong way to use these meditations along your spiritual journey, whether you travel alone or with others. At this point some have been used in traditional worship settings, for small group worship, for devotions on retreats, in hospital worship, and in house churches. Read them, share them. Wrestle with the shadows and emerge in the light.

1

An Invitation to Follow

Jesus called the crowd with his disciples, and said to them, "If any want to become my followers, let them deny themselves and take up their cross and follow me. For those who want to save their life will lose it, and those who lose their life for my sake, and for the sake of the gospel, will save it."

—MARK 8:34–35

ASH WEDNESDAY

"Therefore I tell you, do not worry about your life, what you will eat or what you will drink, or about your body, what you will wear. Is not life more than food, and the body more than clothing? Look at the birds of the air; they neither sow nor reap nor gather into barns, and yet your heavenly Father feeds them. Are you not of more value than they? And can any of you by worrying add a single hour to your span of life? And why do you worry about clothing? Consider the lilies of the field, how they grow; they neither toil nor spin, yet I tell you, even Solomon in all his glory was not clothed like one of these. But if God so clothes the grass of the field, which is alive today and tomorrow is thrown into the oven, will he not much more clothe you—you of little faith? Therefore do not worry, saying, 'What will we eat?' or 'What will we drink?' or 'What will we wear?' For it is the Gentiles who strive for all these things; and indeed your heavenly Father knows that you need all these things. But strive first for the kingdom of God and his righteousness, and all these things will be given to you as well. So do not worry about tomorrow, for tomorrow will bring worries of its own. Today's trouble is enough for today."

—MATTHEW 6:25–34

OPENING WORDS

Come, walk with me a while.

Where are You going?

For a walk. You probably want to come along.

Is it going to be a long walk?

Might be. But you'll be okay.
We'll rest as much as you need.

Maybe I should put shoes on . . .

and change my clothes.

Not really necessary, but you can if you want to.

So I can go barefoot?

Does that mean we're going to the beach?

Maybe the beach, sure.

Don't you know where You are going?

Yeah, I know where I'm going.
I'm just not sure where you're going to find me.

I thought You asked me to go with You.

I did. It's your journey though;
you can choose any path you like.

I'm following you, but I choose the path?

Yes. Are you ready?

But where are we heading and for how long?

You know—into the desert, the wilderness, the darkness
for about forty days.

These are not my favorite places.

Yeah, I know.

Is this necessary?

Like can you live without it?

Yes.

Technically, yes.

But not fully?

Not abundantly.

I'm not sure I'm ready for this.

You don't have to be.

We aren't really going anywhere, are we? I mean . . .

You'll go where you need to go. It's your journey.

Yeah, I suppose so.

But you said, "desert, wilderness, darkness."

Yes, you've been to these places before;
I've seen you there.

But you're telling me I need to go again—

to the chaos and the brokenness and the painful places.

It will be different this time. You go with intention.
Look for the stillness in the chaos,
the healing in the brokenness, and for the hope in the pain.
I will be there.

So how do we begin?

Be still and you will know.

THURSDAY

As they were going along the road, someone said to him, "I will follow you wherever you go." And Jesus said to him, "Foxes have holes, and birds of the air have nests; but the Son of Man has nowhere to lay his head." To another he said, "Follow me." But he said, "Lord, first let me go and bury my father." But Jesus said to him, "Let the dead bury their own dead; but as for you, go and proclaim the kingdom of God." Another said, "I will follow you, Lord; but let me first say farewell to those at my home." Jesus said to him, "No one who puts a hand to the plow and looks back is fit for the kingdom of God."

—LUKE 9:57–62

God has told you, O mortal, what is good; and what does the Lord require of you but to do justice, and to love kindness, and to walk humbly with your God?

—MICAH 6:8

INTEGRITY

At this decision place I think
of all those called to follow You—
fishermen and tax collectors,
 the blind and the visionaries,
 healers and helpmates,
 the broken and forgotten—
women and men from every generation.
 You called them all by name,
 numbering the hairs on their heads.
I wonder how I can be among them.

In the chill of winter
I long for summer.
As the rain streams down
I wish for cloudless skies.
When the horizon is far,
I desire the anonymity of fog.
In the chaos of the storm,
I seek quiet.

I am a study in contrasts—
    the clarity of high noon
    wrapped in the shadows of deep night.
Contentment lies just beyond my grasp.

Spare me from another possibility.
In every direction, another choice,
    another step—true or false remains to be seen.
Potential greets my doubt
    no matter which way I face.
    People come in all their brokenness
    and I believe they can find wholeness—
    not with my words or touch
    but Yours—they need only ask.
Many don't.
And I am always surprised—
and disappointed.
Why is justice such a hard choice for so many?
One of the few things You require . . .

Yes, mistakes, misjudgments,
    wrong choices for right reasons . . .
You wait patiently to offer grace.

Those other times, though—
    when selfish choices are made
    when fear leads to inactivity
    when willful ignorance turns passivity to oppression—
What of these times? people? places?

Do you forgive those who give up
    themselves in pursuit of power?
Do you pardon those who choose
    success over compassion?
Where is the hope for those of us who see
    all things possible but so little probable?

You—the sound of sheer silence
        and
        the voice of the whirlwind
        the One who creates out of nothing
        the One who was fully human while remaining
fully God—

You can bring opposites together
    why not in the human heart?
Surely there is more to be done!
Where is the strength for the weary?
And the home for the outcast?

You know my name and number the hairs on my head.
I will follow and not look back
I need only direction
in the storm or in the silence . . .
Just let me hear.

FRIDAY

Now Jesus was teaching in one of the synagogues on the sabbath. And just then there appeared a woman with a spirit that had crippled her for eighteen years. She was bent over and was quite unable to stand up straight. When Jesus saw her, he called her over and said, "Woman, you are set free from your ailment." When he laid his hands on her, immediately she stood up straight and began praising God. But the leader of the synagogue, indignant because Jesus had cured on the sabbath, kept saying to the crowd, "There are six days on which work ought to be done; come on those days and be cured, and not on the sabbath day." But the Lord answered him and said, "You hypocrites! Does not each of you on the sabbath untie his ox or his donkey from the manger, and lead it away to give it water? And ought not this woman, a daughter of Abraham whom Satan bound for eighteen long years, be set free from this bondage on the sabbath day?" When he said this, all his opponents were put to shame; and the entire crowd was rejoicing at all the wonderful things that he was doing.

—LUKE 13:10–17

I lift up my eyes to the hills—from where will my help come? My help comes from the Lord, who made heaven and earth.

—PSALM 121: 1–2

HEADS UP

Winter holds tightly to spring—
few signs of warmth, of promise,
break through frozen ground.
Hope eludes me while cold
gray fog weaves around my feet
like a stray cat driven by hunger.
I want to lift my eyes,
search for signs of new life,
but I am too tired, overburdened.
This long season of darkness weighs heavily,
a yoke I am unable to bear
alone.

I complain after a season of heaviness—
How hard it must have been for her!
Eighteen years of staring at the ground,
so weighted down by the burden of living
she could not hold her head up.
A spirit crippled her, bent her right over,
left her unable to stand on her own.

You saw her in the crowd, on a Sabbath.
She couldn't have looked you in the eye,
but You must have seen her hidden under that spirit.
She was strong enough to walk,
to come when You called her.
A simple Word,
a light touch,
and she stood straight and tall,
with praise on her lips.

You broke Tradition
to make her whole.
Liberation—a just cause, worthy of risk.
Why are Your people so afraid to follow Your lead?

So many spirits to cripple us,
keep our heads down.
We bend.
We break.
We barely hear Your call.
We honor Tradition more than ourselves,
more than we praise You.
How many of us go through life
seeing even less than the ground under our feet?

Call me out from under this spirit.
I will trade my yoke for Yours.
I will speak Your Word.
Lift the eyes of those who bend.
Free us all to stand tall
and sing Your praise.

SATURDAY

Then someone came to him and said, "Teacher, what good deed must I do to have eternal life?" And he said to him, "Why do you ask me about what is good? There is only one who is good. If you wish to enter into life, keep the commandments." He said to him, "Which ones?" And Jesus said, "You shall not murder; You shall not commit adultery; You shall not steal; You shall not bear false witness; Honor your father and mother; also, You shall love your neighbor as yourself." The young man said to him, "I have kept all these; what do I still lack?" Jesus said to him, "If you wish to be perfect, go, sell your possessions, and give the money to the poor, and you will have treasure in heaven; then come, follow me." When the young man heard this word, he went away grieving, for he had many possessions.

—MATTHEW 19:16–22

You show me the path of life. In your presence there is fullness of joy; in your right hand are pleasures forevermore.

—PSALM 16:11

NEEDLESS THINGS

A nameless man walked away grieving
   did he ever return with empty hands
      ready to follow You?

He was good—faithful to the commandments
   no murder
   no adultery
   no lying
      honoring mother and father
      loving neighbor and self
Goodness
   pure and simple
but not good enough for him
   would he have been good enough for You
      if he had not sought perfection?
Or did you know how he valued himself,
   not able to see without his pretty things?

What would you have me give away if I were to ask?
   Riches do not weigh me down
   Goodness concerns me less than justice
   I try to follow You even when I am lost . . .
What do I lack?

   You would have me take nothing for this journey
   but I carry more than I can bear
   You would not tell me to sell these things
      or give them away
      they have no value
      except in what they take from me

You tell me to set them down
carry them no more
I am struck by grief
    These are not pretty, shiny things
    they devalue all that I am
    standing between me and the image of You
        shameful secrets
        destructive desires
        partial truths
            unrelenting regrets
            unbalancing beliefs
Never good enough
for anyone
but You would take these things from me
    and more—gladly
if I would ask . . .

2

Encountering the Tempter

THEN JESUS was led up by the Spirit into the wilderness to be tempted by the devil. He fasted forty days and forty nights, and afterwards he was famished. The tempter came and said to him, "If you are the Son of God, command these stones to become loaves of bread." But he answered, "It is written, 'One does not live by bread alone, but by every word that comes from the mouth of God.'" Then the devil took him to the holy city and placed him on the pinnacle of the temple, saying to him, "If you are the Son of God, throw yourself down; for it is written, 'He will command his angels concerning you,' and 'On their hands they will bear you up, so that you will not dash your foot against a stone.'" Jesus said to him, "Again it is written, 'Do not put the Lord your God to the test.'" Again, the devil took him to a very high mountain and showed him all the kingdoms of the world and their splendor; and he said to him, "All these I will give you, if you will fall down and worship me." Jesus said to him, "Away with you, Satan! for it is written, 'Worship the Lord your God, and serve only him.'" Then the devil left him, and suddenly angels came and waited on him.

—MATTHEW 4:1–11

FIRST SUNDAY

While Jesus was at Bethany in the house of Simon the leper, as he sat at the table, a woman came with an alabaster jar of very costly ointment of nard, and she broke open the jar and poured the ointment on his head. But some were there who said to one another in anger, "Why was the ointment wasted in this way? For this ointment could have been sold for more than three hundred denarii, and the money given to the poor." And they scolded her. But Jesus said, "Let her alone; why do you trouble her? She has performed a good service for me. For you always have the poor with you, and you can show kindness to them whenever you wish; but you will not always have me. She has done what she could; she has anointed my body beforehand for its burial. Truly I tell you, wherever the good news is proclaimed in the whole world, what she has done will be told in remembrance of her."

—MARK 14:3–9 (SEE ALSO LUKE 7:36–59)

". . . we are the clay, and you are our potter; we are all the work of your hand."

—ISAIAH 64:8

OPENING PRAYER

A jar cracked open,
the scent of unexpected extravagance
flooded the room.

Judgment filled the space
between perception and understanding,
as a woman knelt at your feet
drying her tears.

She had come—
     unbidden
          unwelcome
               unwanted
                    unclean—
in the house of Pharisee or Leper.

All who watched her found her wanting
          missing
how she cleansed and anointed
          You.

But You saw more
than money wasted
and a life dismissed.

How often do we focus on the jar—
caught up in the expectations of the usual,
failing to notice the human
          being
broken open in our midst?

You welcomed her,
accepted her gifts
and found the others wanting.

Your followers today would respond
just as the original twelve,
though You have taught us to see more clearly.

Crack open these clay jars
that you have paid so dearly for.
Open us to the possibilities of extravagance
in the unexpected encounter
with Pharisees
   Lepers
   Prostitutes
   all of today's
      unbidden
         unwelcome
            unwanted
               unclean.

MONDAY

For God's anger is but for a moment; God's favor is for a life-time. Weeping may linger for the night, but joy comes with the morning.

—Psalm 30:5

BEACH LESSONS

After a storm the beach sparkles
    with bits of rocks and shells
    treasures in the eyes of some.
Drawn to shapes and colors on the cold sand
    it's beach glass I am after
    green and brown, mostly, some white
    and the coveted blue, the rare red
Sharp, broken edges worn away
    by water and sand—
    the journey of years.

If sand and glass, waves and wind
    know the secret of beauty,
    why do we resist?
We hide our sharp edges in guilt and
    cover our brokenness with shame.
But could we not benefit from exposure?
    To wear away the sharpness
    reshape the brokenness
    reveal hidden beauty?

TUESDAY

While he was saying these things to them, suddenly a leader of the synagogue came in and knelt before him, saying, "My daughter has just died; but come and lay your hand on her, and she will live." And Jesus got up and followed him, with his disciples. Then suddenly a woman who had been suffering from hemorrhages for twelve years came up behind him and touched the fringe of his cloak, for she said to herself, "If I only touch his cloak, I will be made well." Jesus turned, and seeing her he said, "Take heart, daughter; your faith has made you well." And instantly the woman was made well. When Jesus came to the leader's house and saw the flute players and the crowd making a commotion, he said, "Go away; for the girl is not dead but sleeping." And they laughed at him. But when the crowd had been put outside, he went in and took her by the hand, and the girl got up. And the report of this spread throughout that district.

—MATTHEW 9:18–26

I hold back my feet from every evil way, in order to keep your word.
I do not turn away from your ordinances, for you have taught me.
How sweet are your words to my taste, sweeter than honey to my mouth! Through your precepts I get understanding; therefore I hate every false way.
Your word is a lamp to my feet and a light to my path.
I have sworn an oath and confirmed it, to observe your righteous ordinances.
I am severely afflicted; give me life,
O Lord, according to your word.

—PSALM 119:101–107

WORD SEARCH

words of wisdom fail me
words of hope no longer hold me
words of promise fade away
here I stand
 alone
 wordless
 waiting

a man whose daughter lay near death
a woman pushed to the edge by sickness
both came to You
 one directly
 one discreetly
  both desperately faithful
You gifted them each with new life

long ago I was a daughter who romanced death
 some sought You on my behalf
during the long years of illness
 I couldn't let go of fear long enough
 to reach out to You
but You were there
I did not die

now I stand amidst the shattered remnants of my self
wondering how to make my life new
searching for You
I left behind much that defined
 home and family
  despair and heartache
 work and marriage
  rejection and ill health

not being dead used to be good enough
as I look around this strange, barren land
    marked by the wreckage of damaged dreams and
    forgotten promises
I am certain of needing more

mine is
neither the confident faith of a loving father
nor the undeniable faith of an unseen woman
but I would come to You—as they did—
    directly or discreetly
    but desperately

death retreats into the shadows
as I emerge out of the ruins
You spoke a word and life was restored
    to a beloved daughter
    and an outcast woman
I am somewhere in between
and in need of a Word
find me here
my hands are open

WEDNESDAY

Immediately he made the disciples get into the boat and go on ahead to the other side, while he dismissed the crowds. And after he had dismissed the crowds, he went up the mountain by himself to pray. When evening came, he was there alone, but by this time the boat, battered by the waves, was far from the land, for the wind was against them. And early in the morning he came walking toward them on the sea. But when the disciples saw him walking on the sea, they were terrified, saying, "It is a ghost!" And they cried out in fear. But immediately Jesus spoke to them and said, "Take heart, it is I; do not be afraid." Peter answered him, "Lord, if it is you, command me to come to you on the water." He said, "Come." So Peter got out of the boat, started walking on the water, and came toward Jesus. But when he noticed the strong wind, he became frightened, and beginning to sink, he cried out, "Lord, save me!" Jesus immediately reached out his hand and caught him, saying to him, "You of little faith, why did you doubt?" When they got into the boat, the wind ceased. And those in the boat worshiped him, saying, "Truly you are the Son of God."

—MATTHEW 14:22–33

Awake, awake, put on your strength, O Zion! Put on your beautiful garments, O Jerusalem, the holy city . . . Shake yourself from the dust, rise up, O captive Jerusalem; loose the bonds from your neck, O captive daughter Zion!

—ISAIAH 52:1–2

SELF DEFEAT

Exhaustion.
Waves.
Winds.
    Who would not be afraid?

Darkness.
Changed reality.
A man walking on the sea.
    Who would not tremble?

Those who were in that boat
who had witnessed the extraordinary—
    miracle after miracle
        feeding
        healing
        teaching.
Should they not have known You?
Those who lived with You,
loved You,
followed You—
Why were they so afraid that night?

    And Peter where was your strength?
        what made you let go of the beautiful
            garments of grace to
        grab hold of the bonds that would fearfully
            pull you under?

You left your nets and your family
to follow a carpenter
who rebuilt the way of things.
    You only believed enough for a step or two.

    You could stand in his presence
    defy the laws of nature at his command
        only to be sunk by wind?

Yes, I know that if I were in that boat
I would have done less,
captivated by fear.
I would not have jumped overboard
or even entertained the thought.

    If I had, I, too, would cry out
    as I fell into the cold, dark waters
    misunderstanding whose authority
    guided my steps.

Who among us can criticize?
    Exhaustion
    Wind
    Waves
    Darkness
    and (sometimes) Changed reality.
All familiar things that lead to
    ordinary fear
        and occasional trembling.
If a man walked on water in our line of sight
a "Fear not" would be required.

In all these years since
how have we not managed to
clothe ourselves with strength and beauty,
rise from the dust
in boundless freedom?

Perhaps we ought be still and listen
    until You say, "Come."
Or do we need to cry out in our sinking
    before the waves overwhelm us?
Or maybe we should just open our eyes
    to the beautiful garments of grace freely given . . .

THURSDAY

They came to Jericho. As he and his disciples and a large crowd were leaving Jericho, Bartimaeus son of Timaeus, a blind beggar, was sitting by the roadside. When he heard that it was Jesus of Nazareth, he began to shout out and say, "Jesus, Son of David, have mercy on me!" Many sternly ordered him to be quiet, but he cried out even more loudly, "Son of David, have mercy on me!" Jesus stood still and said, "Call him here." And they called the blind man, saying to him, "Take heart; get up, he is calling you." So throwing off his cloak, he sprang up and came to Jesus. Then Jesus said to him, "What do you want me to do for you?" The blind man said to him, "My teacher, let me see again." Jesus said to him, "Go; your faith has made you well." Immediately he regained his sight and followed him on the way.

—MARK 10:46–52

Blessed are those who trust in the Lord, whose trust is the Lord. They shall be like a tree planted by water, sending out its roots by the stream. It shall not fear when heat comes, and its leaves shall stay green; in the year of drought it is not anxious, and it does not cease to bear fruit.

—JEREMIAH 17:7–8

IN SIGHT

A blind man recognized You and called out for mercy.
A tree bears fruit in the heat of drought.
How have I lost sight of You
when You ask again and again,
"What do you want me to do for you?"

Bartimaeus recognized You, demanded your attention,
and was smart enough to follow you in response
while I complain of clouded vision and fallow years
unaware that You have been there all along
    —waiting, asking.
Did Bartimaeus ever lose his way
    —before or after his sight restored?

How many of us are like trees planted by water
without our knowing?
Years come and go.
The roots grow deeper without notice.
Branches reach upward
sprouting leaves and bearing fruit
in due season.
Yet the trees seem not to know the source
    of their living,
feeling only the heat of drought,
oblivious to the fruit bending their branches.

Yet You stand there still,
asking what You can do for us,
offering living water.

Jesus, Son of David,
In our untrusting blindness, have mercy.
Quiet the anxious with gentle waters,
restore sight to the blind,
and plant trust in the fallow ones.
Call us to the way.

FRIDAY

So he came to a Samaritan city called Sychar, near the plot of ground that Jacob had given to his son Joseph. Jacob's well was there, and Jesus, tired out by his journey, was sitting by the well. It was about noon. A Samaritan woman came to draw water, and Jesus said to her, "Give me a drink." (His disciples had gone to the city to buy food.) The Samaritan woman said to him, "How is it that you, a Jew, ask a drink of me, a woman of Samaria?" (Jews do not share things in common with Samaritans.) Jesus answered her, "If you knew the gift of God, and who it is that is saying to you, 'Give me a drink,' you would have asked him, and he would have given you living water." The woman said to him, "Sir, you have no bucket, and the well is deep. Where do you get that living water? Are you greater than our ancestor Jacob, who gave us the well, and with his sons and his flocks drank from it?" Jesus said to her, "Everyone who drinks of this water will be thirsty again, but those who drink of the water that I will give them will never be thirsty. The water that I will give will become in them a spring of water gushing up to eternal life." The woman said to him, "Sir, give me this water, so that I may never be thirsty or have to keep coming here to draw water." Jesus said to her, "Go, call your husband, and come back." The woman answered him, "I have no husband." Jesus said to her, "You are right in saying, 'I have no husband'; for you have had five husbands, and the one you have now is not your husband. What you have said is true!" The woman said to him, "Sir, I see that you are a prophet. Our ancestors worshiped on this mountain, but you say that the place where people must worship is in Jerusalem." Jesus said to her, "Woman, believe me, the hour is coming when you will worship the Father neither on this mountain nor in Jerusalem. You worship what you do not know; we worship what we know, for salvation is from the Jews. But the hour is coming, and is now here, when the true worshipers will worship the Father in spirit and truth, for the Father seeks such as these to worship him. God is spirit, and those who worship him must worship in spirit and truth." The woman said to him, "I know that Messiah is coming" (who is called Christ). "When he comes, he will proclaim all things to us." Jesus said to her, "I am he, the one who is speaking to you."

—JOHN 4:5–26
(SEE 4:5–42 FOR COMPLETE STORY)

How long, O Lord? Will you forget me forever? How long will you hide your face from me? How long must I bear pain in my soul, and have sorrow in my heart all day long? How long shall my enemy be exalted over me? Consider and answer me, O Lord my God! Give light to my eyes, or I will sleep the sleep of death, and my enemy will say, "I have prevailed;" my foes will rejoice because I am shaken. But I trusted in your steadfast love; my heart shall rejoice in your salvation. I will sing to the Lord, because he has dealt bountifully with me.

—PSALM 13

IN SEARCH OF WELL BEING

How long will You leave me in the desert
with my well running dry
the scorching sun yielding only
barren, parched sand
with no relief in sight?

A woman at a well in the desert at noon
came to draw water
alone
to hide her sins in blinding light
isolated by unbearable heat

cool and calm
You waited for her
knowing what she was
and what she was not

You offered her much
more than her jar could hold
certainly more than she intended to draw
she left the jar behind

You spoke and revealed her truth
courageous and strong she withstood
transforming an outcast among those cast out
into a prophet
speaking Your word right out loud

she who had had five husbands and one more ambiguous
drank of Living Water
drawn from the well of Your being
filled her with insight
into You
into herself

surely I have wandered long enough
sweltering
condemned by those who ought to know better

am I less deserving than a woman whose name history
failed to notice?
if I confess my sins
will You will you pour life into my being?

with words well-spoken
You washed her clean in revealing light
and her eyes were opened
wide enough to see You

she had come with an empty jar
wanting only for water for the day
she was not even looking for You
and You offered her water for life

what did she bring that I have not?
I carry an emptiness that no jar can hold
more barren than the desert with its sun too hot to
bear
and light too bright to see
I am more comfortable in the shadows
where judgment is not so glaring
but there is no well here

You met her in noontime light
nothing hidden
everything revealed
why not here
in the desert I wander?

You filled her being well
and she sang your praises
to those who had refused to see her
until all eyes were on You
I would do no less.
When will I find well being?

SATURDAY

He entered Jericho and was passing through it. A man was there named Zacchaeus; he was a chief tax collector and was rich. He was trying to see who Jesus was, but on account of the crowd he could not, because he was short in stature. So he ran ahead and climbed a sycamore tree to see him, because he was going to pass that way. When Jesus came to the place, he looked up and said to him, "Zacchaeus, hurry and come down; for I must stay at your house today." So he hurried down and was happy to welcome him. All who saw it began to grumble and said, "He has gone to be the guest of one who is a sinner." Zacchaeus stood there and said to the Lord, "Look, half of my possessions, Lord, I will give to the poor; and if I have defrauded anyone of anything, I will pay back four times as much." Then Jesus said to him, "Today salvation has come to this house, because he too is a son of Abraham. For the Son of Man came to seek out and to save the lost."

—LUKE 19:1–10

He shall judge between the nations, and shall arbitrate for many peoples; they shall beat their swords into plowshares, and their spears into pruning hooks; nation shall not lift up sword against nation, neither shall they learn war any more.

—ISAIAH 2:4

IN NEED OF GROUNDING

A small man climbed a sycamore tree
   to get a better view of You.
   Out on a limb, he yearned to see,
   but You called his name.
Before the branch cracked
You broke bread with him.
   For a moment, he looked the fool
   until You brought him to the ground.

      The trees we climb today are not harmless figs.
      They are planted in fear,
      nurtured in greed,
      branching out in power-filled lust.

Security is not peace though
we give it Your name
to fool ourselves.

How long have you stood
patiently calling one name after another,
hoping we hear before another
   branch gives way,
     another life falls
       through the cracks
         in our understanding?

Zacchaeus really wanted to see You for himself.
With war and weapons everywhere,
   hunger permeating every defense,
   sickness in indiscriminant pursuit of life,
   hatred and judgment tarring every nation,

can any of us say that we climb higher
in our artificial trees
to see You for ourselves?

Call us again,
we who call on You.
Remind us that you walked defenseless
to bring us peace—
    peace not as the world gives.
You offered your body broken
    into abundant life.

You saw Zacchaeus before he saw You.
When will we see You before we see other?

Name us.
Ground us
    in Your presence.
        Show us the way down
                from the trees of our foolishness,
                    disarming others along the way
                        joining those who struggle in the search
                            for You.

3

Searching for the Path

In everything do to others as you would have them do to you; for this is the law and the prophets. Enter through the narrow gate; for the gate is wide and the road is easy that leads to destruction, and there are many who take it. For the gate is narrow and the road is hard that leads to life, and there are few who find it.

—MATTHEW 7:12–14

SECOND SUNDAY

After this there was a festival of the Jews, and Jesus went up to Jerusalem. Now in Jerusalem by the Sheep Gate there is a pool, called in Hebrew Beth-zatha, which has five porticoes. In these lay many invalids—blind, lame, and paralyzed. One man was there who had been ill for thirty-eight years. When Jesus saw him lying there and knew that he had been there a long time, he said to him, "Do you want to be made well?" The sick man answered him, "Sir, I have no one to put me into the pool when the water is stirred up; and while I am making my way, someone else steps down ahead of me." Jesus said to him, "Stand up, take your mat and walk." At once the man was made well, and he took up his mat and began to walk.

—JOHN 5:1–9

. . . but those who wait for the Lord shall renew their strength, they shall mount up with wings like eagles, they shall run and not be weary, they shall walk and not faint.

—ISAIAH 40:31

PARTIAL PARALYSIS

Desert surrounds me
Sun, heat, sand—all unrelenting,
unforgiving
as far as I can see.
Between what was and what will be
I remain
unable to take the next step.

I came to this wilderness time
with intent
to seek You out in the emptiness,
longing to hear the sound of You in the stillness.
Yet here I stand
without moving
bound by shades of yesterday.

A man on a mat for thirty-eight years lay
waiting for a miracle in waters stirred up.
He could not move far enough, fast enough
to find wholeness
before the waters quieted and he was left to wait
again.

How long have I lived like him,
lying in brokenness?
I remain unmoved, confined in fear ,
immobilized by doubts,
while those with power
walk all over me.

You showed up and saw him there—
restricted by his body, limited to his mat,
unable to move beyond.
You assumed nothing of him
and asked if he wanted to be made well.
He explained his predicament but did not answer
directly.

You watch me limit myself
each day a repetition of routine—
wanting wholeness and never quite
getting there.
You ask if I, too, want to be made well.
My answer is no more direct.

You healed him anyway
with a direction to walk.
Did You see in him more than a
body broken?
What did his words hold out to you?

If I were to take up this mat of mine—
woven by others who would keep me still—
where would I go?
Did that man ever miss
knowing the limits of his life?
How did he bear sudden wholeness?
I'm not sure I'm strong enough
to walk away with You.

The man was paralyzed, at least in part,
yet he heard Your call to life quite clearly.
Was there a hesitation
between the Word and re-action?

New life surged through his being
as he believed
he could take up his mat and walk
toward all things possible.

Most days, I wait for the miracle
and long for the stillness of knowing
I can make my way to the waters
if I so choose.
But I cannot quite believe
Your call is enough to set me free from all that binds.

Forgive me.
I want to be made well,
to take those first trembling steps
and bear the weight of my doubt
here in the midst of my imperfect life
bound to a mat woven
with so little justice.

I wait in this shaded spot.
Give me direction.

MONDAY

Why are you cast down, O my soul, and why are you disquieted within me? Hope in God; for I shall again praise him, my help and my God.

—Psalm 42:11

SPRING STORM

Bleak, dark sky promising more snow greets me
with chilled silence as I step out tonight.
No stars, just clouds for the storm that will be
tomorrow's destiny. Darkness, no light,
outside or in, as I walk sleeping streets.
Restless, weary, uncertain, I seek more
hope—an end to despair and self-defeat—
a new sense that You have a purpose for
my being. Maybe this storm is the last
of the season. I turn toward home, echoes
follow me—footsteps, thoughts, dark shadows past
and present. You may know where my path goes,
I do not. But winds taste of springtime snow
which will melt into the life I will know.

TUESDAY

You are the light of the world. A city built on a hill cannot
be hid. No one after lighting a lamp puts it under the bushel
basket, but on the lampstand, and it gives light to all in the
house. In the same way, let your light shine before others, so
that they may see your good works and give glory to your
Father in heaven.

—MATTHEW 5:14–16

God uncovers the deeps out of darkness, and brings deep
darkness to light.

—JOB 12:22

LESSONS FROM STAR ISLAND SUNRISE

I sit on the edge of night
   anticipating the day's first light.
      Waves wash gently over rocks
         seals splash just beyond my view.
            While restless thoughts fill me
         stars fade from sight
      and crimson spreads across the horizon
separating water and sky.

Gulls herald the coming of day
as reds reach into orange
   pulling the sun out of ocean depths
      to set fire to the night
         burning away all darkness
            casting rich colors on the shore.

I stand in this new light
filled with longing
for the sun to warm
the deep dark within me
until the fires of morning
hope ignite possibility
opening the promise of
more than the lingering dark.

The sun lifts into newly blue sky
warming air, rocks, and waves
saturating all with light
drawing out natural colors
shapes and shadows.

Stepping into the sun
deep darkness ebbs
as I welcome light
embrace the day
giving thanks.

WEDNESDAY

They came to Bethsaida. Some people brought a blind man to him and begged him to touch him. He took the blind man by the hand and led him out of the village; and when he had put saliva on his eyes and laid his hands on him, he asked him, "Can you see anything?" And the man looked up and said, "I can see people, but they look like trees, walking." Then Jesus laid his hands on his eyes again; and he looked intently and his sight was restored, and he saw everything clearly.

—MARK 8:22–25

O Lord, all my longing is known to you; my sighing is not hidden from you.

—PSALM 38:9

A PRAYER FOR CLARITY
IN EARLY SPRING

fog and ocean blend together
mixing ground and horizon
night clings loosely to day
as I sit wrapped in gray
waiting for sunrise

predawn blue merges with
low clouds limiting my vision
I can see neither before nor behind
my feet fade into wet grays of winter sand
lost but for my red shoes

when I have needed You
I've found You here in ocean flow
You speak in the swell of water and wind
in the coolness of salt-laden air
You make Your presence known

island–born in a land–locked family
I need ocean ebb and flow—
freedom, light, hope—
a sense of You

today I come knowing the limits of my sight
caught in the chaos pretending to be life
blinded by the hands of others
who would lead me away

winter fog fills me
washes out all color
distorts my senses
leaves me with trees walking

touch me again
even as the sun pulls day from night
burning away the clouds
let me emerge from the gray
with more color and clarity
than just my red shoes

THURSDAY

Now as they went on their way, he entered a certain village, where a woman named Martha welcomed him into her home. She had a sister named Mary, who sat at the Lord's feet and listened to what he was saying. But Martha was distracted by her many tasks; so she came to him and asked, "Lord, do you not care that my sister has left me to do all the work by myself? Tell her then to help me." But the Lord answered her, "Martha, Martha, you are worried and distracted by many things; there is need of only one thing. Mary has chosen the better part, which will not be taken away from her."

—LUKE 10:38–42

You show me the path of life. In your presence there is fullness of joy; in your right hand are pleasures forevermore.

—PSALM 16:11

THE BETTER PART

Show me this path of life
    that leads to fullness of joy
        in the pleasures of your presence.

        I want to sit as Mary sat
        at Your feet
        listening
        hearing
        knowing.

By another's account
   Martha clearly saw
      what others could not
         and recognized You
in her moment of loss and despair.

         How could her everyday distractions
         turn her attention from sitting with You?

         What did it matter
         that her house was not clean
         and dinner was late
         when You walked through her door?

         Did she worry about disappointing You
         so much that she forgot You
         accept her—no perfection
            of house, food, or self
            required?

How did Mary know
   to be still
   and listen?

         What did she hear that Martha did not?

         Walk through my door today.
        Call me from my tasks.
         The worries and distractions of my day
       drown out the still
       small voice of You.

Pursuing perfection
demands more than I want to give
with too great a price.

Show me Your path
to let go of worry and distraction
to know what is needful
and to choose the better part.

FRIDAY

The scribes and the Pharisees brought a woman who had been caught in adultery; and making her stand before all of them, they said to him, "Teacher, this woman was caught in the very act of committing adultery. Now in the law Moses commanded us to stone such women. Now what do you say?" They said this to test him, so that they might have some charge to bring against him. Jesus bent down and wrote with his finger on the ground. When they kept on questioning him, he straightened up and said to them, "Let anyone among you who is without sin be the first to throw a stone at her." And once again he bent down and wrote on the ground. When they heard it, they went away, one by one, beginning with the elders; and Jesus was left alone with the woman standing before him. Jesus straightened up and said to her, "Woman, where are they? Has no one condemned you?" She said, "No one, sir." And Jesus said, "Neither do I condemn you. Go your way, and from now on do not sin again."

—JOHN 8:3–11

The Lord is near to the brokenhearted, and saves the crushed in spirit.

—PSALM 34:18

SEASON CHANGE

Despair wraps around me
like a blizzard
   blinding snow
   disorienting winds
   fierce cold
bringing an isolating darkness
with the threat
of never ending.

What hope will guide my feet
when each step gives way to new loss?
Once, I was sure I heard You calling,
now I hear only stormy silence.

This path under my feet
was supposed to lead to You.
Yet here I am—deep in the wilderness.

   She must have felt much the same
   when they dropped her at Your feet—
   glaringly alone
   without much hope, if any,
   for her life.

   Those who would condemn
   turned away as you rocked
   their understanding.
   Was she able to pick herself up
   from despair
   to walk back into the life You
   restored to her?

No stones were thrown that day . . .
You lifted the weight of condemnation.
Where did it fall?
  Back on her,
  on those who held rocks at the ready,
  or down through the ages to settle into the hearts
  of those who pass judgment in Your name?

If I look up from this dreary path,
will I stumble onto You?
When I find myself at your feet,
speak the words
  to dismiss the condemnation that echoes
    through my life,
  heal the heartbreak that binds me to despair,
  and allow me to go and sin no more
    as wintery blizzards give way to
    gentle spring rains.

SATURDAY

People were bringing little children to him in order that he might touch them; and the disciples spoke sternly to them. But when Jesus saw this, he was indignant and said to them, "Let the little children come to me; do not stop them; for it is to such as these that the kingdom of God belongs. Truly I tell you, whoever does not receive the kingdom of God as a little child will never enter it." And he took them up in his arms, laid his hands on them, and blessed them.

—MARK 6:7–13

The law of the Lord is perfect, reviving the soul; the decrees of the Lord are sure, making wise the simple; the precepts of the Lord are right, rejoicing the heart; the commandment of the Lord is clear, enlightening the eyes; the fear of the Lord is pure, enduring forever; the ordinances of the Lord are true and righteous altogether. More to be desired are they than gold, even much fine gold; sweeter also than honey, and drippings of the honeycomb.

—PSALM 19:7–10

EARLY SPRING DREAMS

Paths through childhood woods
lace my dreams these late winter nights
   winding through pine and fern
   around granite boulders and thickets of thorn
   connecting my street to the next one over
   no road needed on any given day.

Shadows became monsters at dusk
and rocks were suspected trolls
hurrying our scurrying feet toward home
after a long day of imaginary encounters.

All seasons had their purpose in those woods
    summers of tree houses and fairy teas
    autumns of hide-and-seek and falling leaves
    winters of building forts and throwing snowballs
    and spring with its hunts for first flowers—
        the patch of violets slightly off the path
        lady slippers hidden in the patch of ferns
        Indian pipes just the other side of the boulder
        and snapdragons in unpredictable places . . .

Those paths were simple,
    warn by small feet and bicycle tires,
requiring no map and little thought of direction.

My feet have encountered nothing quite so simple
since those woods gave way to houses.

    Now that I am on my way through
        this unfamiliar place
        between what was and what might be,
        I want to take nothing more
            than the expectation of adventure.
                I've missed too many fairy teas and snow forts
                and lady slippers and Indian pipes.
                All these would have been forgotten
                    if not for dreaming.

Let me shake the dust off my travel-weary feet
and open my eyes to the wonders of this path
(shadow monsters, rock trolls, included)

4

Shadows in the Darkness

Immediately he made his disciples get into the boat and go on ahead to the other side, to Bethsaida, while he dismissed the crowd. After saying farewell to them, he went up on the mountain to pray. When evening came, the boat was out on the sea, and he was alone on the land. When he saw that they were straining at the oars against an adverse wind, he came towards them early in the morning, walking on the sea. He intended to pass them by. But when they saw him walking on the sea, they thought it was a ghost and cried out; for they all saw him and were terrified. But immediately he spoke to them and said, "Take heart, it is I; do not be afraid." Then he got into the boat with them and the wind ceased. And they were utterly astounded . . .

—MARK 6:45–51

THIRD SUNDAY

He said to them, "Because of your little faith. For truly I tell you, if you have faith the size of a mustard seed, you will say to this mountain, 'Move from here to there,' and it will move; and nothing will be impossible for you."

—MATTHEW 17:20

As a deer longs for flowing streams, so my soul longs for you, O God. My soul thirsts for God, for the living God. When shall I come and behold the face of God?

—PSALM 42:1–2

MUSTARD SEED PRAYER

If I had this mustard seed faith
could I remove this mountainous doubt
and step out from under into light?
You—I believe; me—I don't trust.
I've been broken beyond being whole—
fractured, bruised, pained—in need of grace.

Kneeling, unable to stand, I ask for grace
so I may leap forward, offering faith
in return. Fill this gaping hole,
remove this cavernous, formless doubt
that undermines hope and swallows trust.
Acquainted with night, I long for the light

of You. Speak a Word to make my path light,
heal my brokenness; I will proclaim Your grace
to all who have ears. Now I wander—distrust
weighing heavily on budding faith—
easily distracted by gods of doubt,
the voices of shattered hopes. I would be whole

and wholly Yours. Can I ever be whole
enough to let go of dark and walk in light?
No question of what I need, no doubt—
Your forgiving, healing, boundless grace,
a seed to nurture, cultivate into faith
with strong, deep roots reaching for trust.

With You all things are possible, even trust
where only despair has been. A whole
new life re-created, re-shaped by faith
in You. Dark bruises, old fractures, turn to light
while fear and anxiety whither before grace.
How long before this seed grows stronger than doubt?

Will you satisfy this consuming doubt—
cleanse me of this dark, destructive distrust
of myself? This seed, how much grace
does it need before I can look into this hole
and see a reflection of You—light
where emptiness has been? In You I place faith.

At Your feet I drop doubt, longing to be whole.
Gift me with trust enough to walk in light,
bear Your grace, plant seeds of faith.

MONDAY

Now there was a Pharisee named Nicodemus, a leader of the
Jews. He came to Jesus by night and said to him, "Rabbi, we
know that you are a teacher who has come from God; for
no one can do these signs that you do apart from the presence of God." Jesus answered him, "Very truly, I tell you, no
one can see the kingdom of God without being born from
above." Nicodemus said to him, "How can anyone be born
after having grown old? Can one enter a second time into the
mother's womb and be born?" Jesus answered, "Very truly, I
tell you, no one can enter the kingdom of God without being
born of water and Spirit. What is born of the flesh is flesh,
and what is born of the Spirit is spirit. Do not be astonished
that I said to you, 'You must be born from above.' The wind
blows where it chooses, and you hear the sound of it, but you
do not know where it comes from or where it goes. So it is
with everyone who is born of the Spirit." Nicodemus said to
him, "How can these things be?" Jesus answered him, "Are
you a teacher of Israel, and yet you do not understand these
things? "Very truly, I tell you, we speak of what we know
and testify to what we have seen; yet you do not receive our
testimony. If I have told you about earthly things and you
do not believe, how can you believe if I tell you about heavenly things? No one has ascended into heaven except the one
who descended from heaven, the Son of Man. And just as
Moses lifted up the serpent in the wilderness, so must the
Son of Man be lifted up, that whoever believes in him may
have eternal life." For God so loved the world that he gave his
only Son, so that everyone who believes in him may not per-
ish but may have eternal life. "Indeed, God did not send the
Son into the world to condemn the world, but in order that
the world might be saved through him. Those who believe
in him are not condemned; but those who do not believe are

condemned already, because they have not believed in the name of the only Son of God. And this is the judgment, that the light has come into the world, and people loved darkness rather than light because their deeds were evil. For all who do evil hate the light and do not come to the light, so that their deeds may not be exposed. But those who do what is true come to the light, so that it may be clearly seen that their deeds have been done in God."

—JOHN 3:1–21

If I say, "Surely the darkness shall cover me, and the light around me become night," even the darkness is not dark to you; the night is as bright as day for the darkness is as light to you.

—PSALM 139:11–12

REMINISCENT OF NICODEMUS

How many have come to You in the night—
cloaked with shadows, shaded by sins,
real and imagined?

One who walked in darkness came to You.
Did he see a great light?

History claims Nicodemus was afraid of what others would think,
didn't want to be seen by judging eyes.

I like to think he was hiding from himself,
not wanting to admit his arrogance or his need,
afraid You would leave him alone—
unworthy to walk in the Light.

Born of darkness,
shaped by secrets,
I am a child of shadows—
unwanted, unknown,
frequently unseen.

Maybe Nicodemus was, too.
He had a perfect life—
a position of power,
a place of respect,
a proper son of Abraham.
But he needed something more.

One night he stepped out of the shadows
to ask about the Light.
You gave him answers
too bright for him to bear.
He took your words,
bundled them up for later use.

How many nights have I come to You?
Holding my secrets
as if You couldn't see . . .
Whispering my need
as if You couldn't hear . . .
Asking for more . . .

Shadows are not enough.
Power, respect, propriety—
all safe and desirable, acceptable even.
But they leave an emptiness that can only be filled
with
Darkness or
Light.

Nicodemus knew.
He walked through the night
to carry out the Light.

He traded comfort, predictability
for the winds of the Spirit
that would blow the shadows out of his life—
a little at a time as he pondered the Word.

I want what Nicodemus got—
Courage to walk from yesterday into today.

No keeper of Tradition,
I am not enamored with power or place.
This lifetime of night-time,
I could do without.

So I come like Nicodemus did—
in the night, tired of darkness,
asking, pleading . . .
Give me the Word that will illumine me,
cast out the shadows—real and imagined—
Set me free,
to do as Nicodemus did.

TUESDAY

Do not remember the former things, or consider the things of old. I am about to do a new thing; now it springs forth, do you not perceive it? I will make a way in the wilderness and rivers in the desert.

—ISAIAH 43:18–19

OASIS

trees shimmer on the far horizon
the smell of water floats on dusty air
my feet trudge through blistering sand
I wonder where this journey will lead

the desert, the wild places, are full of shadows
tantalizing with the promise of cool respite
but shade vanishes in the bright sun
and rest is an illusion of my own weary thoughts

until it rains in the mountains and the cities
making rivers flow through the desert
where only dry, dead ground had been
just minutes before

I sit watching the ochre waters flow
mesmerized by the sudden power
of gathering rain on its way to the sea
taking barren ground with it

I breathe the rhythm of the rushing rivers
the stillness of the hot sand holds me
light fills me
darkness leaves me

You entrance me with visions of what could be
if I complete the journey through the dark, dry,
broken, forgotten wilderness of my being
peace falls on me with the first drops of desert rain

life stirs
endless dusty miles burst into green
unexpected growth
thriving

I rise and walk
discovering the horizon has moved closer
the sand no longer burns
I am where the journey ends

WEDNESDAY

Once when Jesus was praying alone, with only the disciples near him, he asked them, "Who do the crowds say that I am?" They answered, "John the Baptist; but others, Elijah; and still others, that one of the ancient prophets has arisen." He said to them, "But who do you say that I am?" Peter answered, "The Messiah of God."

—LUKE 9:18–20

O sing to the Lord a new song; sing to the Lord, all the earth. Sing to the Lord, bless his name; tell of his salvation from day to day.

—PSALM 96:1–2

MOMENT OF TRUTH

In that moment of answer
    Peter was as sure as ever
        he could be.
Did he hesitate in his proclamation
    like he sank in the water
        cut off a servant's ear
            denied You?
Or was it a moment of truth
    certainty
        without a doubt
            to cloud his understanding
a moment of pure insight?

You confused the crowds
with Your words
Your power
Your being
then and now.

They thought You were
John or Elijah or some other
prophet returned to them.

Centuries later the question still echoes
and the answers remain the same
mostly
prophet
philosopher
spiritual guide
sometimes Messiah
though not without doubt.

Do You wonder why so many hesitate
sink in overwhelming waters
cut off so much more than a servant's ear
and deny even the thought of You?

I do.
I wonder at myself
when I think about You
what I would say in response
to Your question
knowing that I can only hold
the fullness of You

for a moment or two
before I fall from the grace
of knowing into the certainty
of doubt.

You lived a new song
and the lyrics still echo
here and there
when we are attuned to You
we might hear "Messiah of God."
Your words
Your power
Your being
now and then
step away from the crowds
to stand with Peter
in his moment of insight
to tell of Your salvation
today.

THURSDAY

Soon afterwards he went on through cities and villages, proclaiming and bringing the good news of the kingdom of God. The twelve were with him, as well as some women who had been cured of evil spirits and infirmities: Mary, called Magdalene, from whom seven demons had gone out, and Joanna, the wife of Herod's steward Chuza, and Susanna, and many others, who provided for them out of their resources.

—LUKE 8:1–3

Out of the depths I cry to you, O Lord. Lord, hear my voice! Let your ears be attentive to the voice of my supplications! If you, O Lord, should mark iniquities, Lord, who could stand? But there is forgiveness with you, so that you may be revered. I wait for the Lord, my soul waits, and in his word I hope; my soul waits for the Lord more than those who watch for the morning, more than those who watch for the morning. O Israel, hope in the Lord! For with the Lord there is steadfast love, and with him is great power to redeem. It is he who will redeem Israel from all its iniquities.

—PSALM 130

MARY OF MAGDALA

In this chilly season of change
I find myself thinking of those who first followed You.
The ones who turned from all things familiar
to walk with You into life transformed.

Of all those first disciples,
Mary of Magdala is one I wish to know.
She who was broken, at least in seven parts,
before she encountered You.

You freed her of her demons—
she became Your witness.
I'm betting there were others,
who went on their way much as before . . .

History offers much speculation about Mary—
    a prostitute reformed
    Your lover when you succumbed to temptation
    Your wife to clean up the implication
    Mother of Your children to entertain novelists of
more than one generation.

Whatever connected her to you
    be it gratitude or love—
        eros, philios, or agape–
matters less than the facts we know.
You trusted her to bear witness
    to life
    to death
    to resurrection.

Demons cast out made her whole.
   I wonder what possessed her . . .

Was she like me—
   broken before wholeness took root?
     Victim of others who couldn't see her
    didn't see her
      only used her
        to sooth themselves?

You healed her, set her free
and she followed you
from death to life.
Seemingly without regrets.

   These are my demons
   and they are more than seven
   though not quite legion.

She who went from outcast to honor
   from one unseen
     to one whose witness
       remains visible.

   How do I grasp Your forgiveness
   as surely as she did?

For Your sake, I would leave
   the chill of this regrettable season
and enter the warmth of your steadfast love.
I watch for morning,
   hoping for the breaking of the day.

FRIDAY

I came that they may have life, and have it abundantly.

—JOHN 10:10

O sing to the Lord a new song; sing to the Lord, all the earth.

—PSALM 96:1

MOUNTAINOUS SPRING

sleeping giants awaken
throw off their blankets of snow
wriggle watery toes
yawn and stretch
unfurl in the sun's new warmth

ice cracks
streams and rivers overflow
crocuses and snowdrops blossom
   inches from frozen ground

birds raise their voices from every branch and bush
squirrels run with seeming abandon
life bursts from every direction

winter was long and dreary
   still lurking in the shadows
    not quite ready to let go
     of mountains
       rivers
         forests

everything frozen
  silent
    still
      dead

  but the sun returns without fail
  life unheard for many months
  sings right out loud

creation remembers what we forget
no matter how long, how hard, how cold the winter
spring always returns
life erupts
  new
    surprising
      abundant

SATURDAY

On that day, when evening had come, he said to them, "Let us go across to the other side." And leaving the crowd behind, they took him with them in the boat, just as he was. Other boats were with him. A great windstorm arose, and the waves beat into the boat, so that the boat was already being swamped. But he was in the stern, asleep on the cushion; and they woke him up and said to him, "Teacher, do you not care that we are perishing?" He woke up and rebuked the wind, and said to the sea, "Peace! Be still!" Then the wind ceased, and there was a dead calm. He said to them, "Why are you afraid? Have you still no faith?" And they were filled with great awe and said to one another, "Who then is this, that even the wind and the sea obey him?"

—MARK 4:35–41

O God, do not keep silence; do not hold your peace or be still, O God!

—PSALM 83:1

A BOAT IN THE STORM

Winds swirl. Clouds collect. Thunder threatens. One
more storm gathers to throw rain and call up swells.
Waves toy with boats—sun and clear sky undone.
My oars slip their locks. Adrift. No one tells
me how to reach safe harbor. Fog nestles
into all things. Distorting. Distressing.
Fear and winds torment. This storm unsettles
quiet demons dormant within. Nothing

points in hope's direction until You wake
and bring the winds, waves, wildness to dead calm.
Stillness. I hear words spoken for my sake.
Fear. Fog. Failure. Evaporate. A balm,
like no other, to heal and forgive. "Peace!
Be still!" I am. You are in this boat. Peace.

5

The Journey Back

Jesus said to her, "Your brother will rise again." Martha said to him, "I know that he will rise again in the resurrection on the last day." Jesus said to her, "I am the resurrection and the life. Those who believe in me, even though they die, will live, and everyone who lives and believes in me will never die. Do you believe this?" She said to him, "Yes, Lord, I believe that you are the Messiah, the Son of God, the one coming into the world."

—John 11:23–27

FOURTH SUNDAY

In those days Jesus came from Nazareth of Galilee and was baptized by John in the Jordan. And just as he was coming up out of the water, he saw the heavens torn apart and the Spirit descending like a dove on him. And a voice came from heaven, "You are my Son, the Beloved; with you I am well pleased."

—MARK 1:9–11

O give thanks to the Lord, for he is good; for his steadfast love endures forever.

—1 CHRONICLES 16:34

NEW THOUGHTS

if I am beloved
    as You are beloved
            then why this gnawing void
            that whispers of nothing
            and threatens all possibilities?

    was it easy for You to cloak Yourself
            with love
            let it flow into
            Your being
            as the Jordan's waters
            washed over You?

as spring approaches
I stand at another river
watching ice thaw into
rushing waters

no prophet stands here
no sky rending
no thunder booming
no voice echoing through the heavens
or anywhere else

I am no one's beloved
yet
this unrest I feel
keeping rhythm with
melting snow
would have me believe
otherwise

the possibility of standing
with You
in You
enters the emptiness
lights the darkness
reshapes
reforms
me
opening my eyes
to see as You see

at the end of this wilderness journey
will my vision clear
will the lingering dark give way
to the flowing waters?

Beloved?
if You
then I . . .

MONDAY

Then Jesus told them a parable about their need to pray always and not to lose heart. He said, "In a certain city there was a judge who neither feared God nor had respect for people. In that city there was a widow who kept coming to him and saying, "Grant me justice against my opponent.' For a while he refused; but later he said to himself, "Though I have no fear of God and no respect for anyone, yet because this widow keeps bothering me, I will grant her justice, so that she may not wear me out by continually coming.' " And the Lord said, "Listen to what the unjust judge says. And will not God grant justice to his chosen ones who cry to him day and night? Will he delay long in helping them? I tell you, he will quickly grant justice to them. And yet, when the Son of Man comes, will he find faith on earth?"

—LUKE 18:1–8

O my God, I cry by day, but you do not answer; and by night, but find no rest.

—PSALM 22:2

PRAYERFUL CONSIDERATION

My standard way of being is to accept what is offered
to collect the crumbs and be thankful
to make something out of nothing
savor little bits of what could be.
No more.

I am too hungry to search out crumbs
waiting for them to fall from the table of the chosen.
So I turn my attention to another—

a woman who was not afraid to seek, ask and
expect a response.

I will be the one who perfects the art of pestering
I will persist and persevere,
stay until You hear me and respond
with more than the minimum required
to get through.

No, I am not greedy.
I've just given away more than I have received.
Now I can't hope for a tomorrow different from
the tomorrows already gone by.

Yes, I have managed and usually found gratitude
enough.
If I am included in Your love
then surely You love me enough to invite me
to sit at the table—
no more waiting underneath for whatever may fall
unwanted by anyone else.

I'm not practiced in the art of
        nagging . . . pestering . . . begging
Knocking on a door makes me nervous,
but my need is now greater than my fear
so I'm asking . . . seeking . . . knocking . . .
and I am not going way with less—
Not again.
I'll wait for You,
but if You were expecting quiet
You have only Yourself to blame.

TUESDAY

Do not fear, for I am with you, do not be afraid, for I am your God; I will strengthen you, I will help you, I will uphold you with my victorious right hand.

—ISAIAH 41:10

Teach me your way, O Lord, that I may walk in your truth; give me an undivided heart to revere your name.

—PSALM 86:11

FEARLESS:
a prayer for an undivided heart

When it comes to fear
    I could do with less.
Yes, I will stand for justice,
    speak for those without voice,
    I will risk myself for another's sake
but make no mistake,
    Fearless is not my name.

Fear wrapped around me at birth
    held me tightly bound to silence
    while darkness filled me,
        defined me
        left me alone
        in trembling despair.

I learned at the hands of others
>> to cower in corners
>> keep silent and hidden.
Lessons in brokenness
>> taught me of power not mine
>> and crammed me full of emptiness.

When I could run no further from myself
You spoke my name, a quiet whisper,
a little flicker of light in the shadows.
You called again and again and again
and I have followed
>> often in reluctance
>> and not without fear
>> in spite of Your "Fear not."

Walking this path of serving and being served
>> I have stumbled and fallen
>>> with amazing frequency.
>> But when darkness threatens
>>> Your light shines.
Yes, I will go where you lead
But I am not without fear.
You, I trust even when I don't understand.
Remember that I bear the scars
>> of those early lessons from human hands.
Have patience when courage fails me
>> and the voices of yesterday echo in my ears.

Until the cry for justice
>> a need for kindness
gives me the strength for one more step.

You have led me here
Walk with me now
    through the waters
        rising and falling
    the fires
        destroying and warming
    the darkness
        threatening and restful
    the wilderness
        chaotic and transforming
through whatever may come

Without You
    I have no voice
        and fear divides my heart.

WEDNESDAY

When it was evening on that day, the first day of the week, and the doors of the house where the disciples had met were locked for fear of the Jews, Jesus came and stood among them and said, "Peace be with you." After he said this, he showed them his hands and his side. Then the disciples rejoiced when they saw the Lord. Jesus said to them again, "Peace be with you. As the Father has sent me, so I send you." When he had said this, he breathed on them and said to them, "Receive the Holy Spirit. If you forgive the sins of any, they are forgiven them; if you retain the sins of any, they are retained."

—JOHN 20:19–23

For the Lord is good; his steadfast love endures forever, and his faithfulness to all generations.

—PSALM 100:5

SUN RISE

I've come to the ocean in the pre-dawn light
hoping to find You
hoping to find myself

In this season of between
    winter and spring
    dark and light
    cold and warmth
    confession and forgiveness
there is something fragile in the human spirit

Into my hands many have poured their needs
    forgiveness of sins long forgotten by others
    hope enough to face blinding despair
    courage to hold fast as death approaches
words of assurance beyond my knowing

Today I carry these burdens of Your people
    to this moment before dawn
        this time between night and day
            when the world is bathed in blue
and ask You to wash them away

Always I wait to the point of breaking
before coming to You as if I didn't know
better

My hands
    in those moments between
        confession and forgiveness
        despair and hope
        death and courage
        words and assurance
are Yours

Forgive my tendency to hold too much
to wait too long
I get caught between the shadows and the light
needlessly

As the sun rises
fulfilling the promise of a new day
I let go of the night
find assurance without words
as blue gives way to imperceptible gold

THURSDAY

Jesus sat down opposite the treasury, and watched the crowd putting money into the treasury. Many rich people put in large sums. A poor widow came and put in two small copper coins, which are worth a penny. Then he called his disciples and said to them, "Truly I tell you, this poor widow has put in more than all those who are contributing to the treasury. For all of them have contributed out of their abundance; but she out of her poverty has put in everything she had, all she had to live on."

—MARK 12:41–44

A WIDOW'S WISDOM

a simple offering
outweighed all others

combined
two copper coins

almost without value
took on significance

she gave to You
all she had

with intent
others offered bits

pieces of notable
value

thinking they honor You
and themselves

giving what they will not miss
in abundance

they missed
abundantly

the widow's gift
lies unseen today

many cling to little
in hopes of more

or less
fear of losing

everything of importance
but gaining nothing of value

Your words were simple
directed at Your followers

then and now
witnesses to You

two worthless coins
mean everything

when there is nothing else
to give

true life requires giving
to You

      in abundance
      without fear of emptiness

      with trust and gratitude
      for You offer

      life
      abundant

      where two small coins
      have value

      and one poor woman
      has purpose

      and wisdom
      blessing

      any and all who see her
      as You did

      giving every little bit
      for the possibility

You hold out
to any and all

who give You
two copper coins

(or everything we have
and everything we are)

FRIDAY

"Which commandment is the first of all?" Jesus answered, "The first is, 'Hear, O Israel: the Lord our God, the Lord is one; you shall love the Lord your God with all your heart, and with all your soul, and with all your mind, and with all your strength.' The second is this, 'You shall love your neighbor as yourself.' There is no other commandment greater than these."

—Mark 12:28a-31

For everything there is a season, and a time for every matter under heaven: a time to be born, and a time to die; a time to plant, and a time to pluck up what is planted; a time to kill, and a time to heal; a time to break down, and a time to build up; a time to weep, and a time to laugh; a time to mourn, and a time to dance; a time to throw away stones, and a time to gather stones together; a time to embrace, and a time to refrain from embracing; a time to seek, and a time to lose; a time to keep, and a time to throw away; a time to tear, and a time to sew; a time to keep silence, and a time to speak; a time to love, and a time to hate; a time for war, and a time for peace.

—Ecclesiastes 3:1–8

A MODERN LAMENT

Those who came before—
In the face of pain, fear, chaos—
asked
HOW LONG?

I am tempted to do the same
but the answer holds no comfort.

One who was plagued by pestilence and grief
    cursed the day he was born and
                demanded
        WHY?
I sympathize
but will not ask
for the response is ever the same . . .
        WHY NOT?

An early philosopher observed
there is nothing new under the sun.
Though several thousand years have passed
I am inclined to agree.
Others may not
        BUT
what happens when we encounter
        difference
            change
                other?
        We hate.
        We fear.
            We kill . . .
often in the name of our god who is
        biggest,
            strongest, fiercest.

When will we learn that there is only
        ONE
        with many names . . .

SATURDAY

"So I say to you, Ask, and it will be given you; search and you will find; knock and the door will be opened for you. For everyone who asks receives, and everyone who searches finds, and for everyone who knocks the door will be opened."

—LUKE 11:9–10

This God—his way is perfect; the promise of the Lord proves true; he is a shield for all who take refuge in him. For who is God, but the Lord? And who is a rock, except our God? The God who has girded me with strength has opened wide my path.

—2 SAMUEL 22:31–33

WIDE OPEN PATH

The first few steps I took into the wilderness
were a near hopeless effort to find new life
in You, in me.
The heat of the desert sun seemed
unbearable
and the shadows of the wild
appeared untamable.

You called.
I followed
not sure where You were leading
or if I should even try one more time.
I have traveled through the desert—
exhausted, confronted
with the vast emptiness
and the potentials of oasis.

Accepting the limits of the climate
I walked on
into memories of mountainous
proportions
running wild through the
center of my life
chilling, clinging
to darkness
denying the promise
of healing.

I cried out to You
and You gave me rest.
Now I breathe deeply
preparing for the end of this
wandering time.

No doubt that I will
lose the path again
and You will call me back
again.
In the meantime
I will walk with You,
washing away the barren places,
lighting the dark edges,
opening wide the path
to hope and healing.

The dessert heat
and wilderness shadows
lose intensity as I walk away
from them and into
the new life unfolding before me.

6

Approaching the Horizon

"Do not let your hearts be troubled. Believe in God, believe also in me. In my Father's house there are many dwelling places. If it were not so, would I have told you that I go to prepare a place for you? And if I go and prepare a place for you, I will come again and will take you to myself, so that where I am, there you may be also. And you know the way to the place where I am going." Thomas said to him, "Lord, we do not know where you are going. How can we know the way?" Jesus said to him, "I am the way, and the truth, and the life.

—JOHN 14:1–6A

SUNDAY

On another sabbath he entered the synagogue and taught, and there was a man there whose right hand was withered. The scribes and the Pharisees watched him to see whether he would cure on the sabbath, so that they might find an accusation against him. Even though he knew what they were thinking, he said to the man who had the withered hand, "Come and stand here." He got up and stood there. Then Jesus said to them, "I ask you, is it lawful to do good or to do harm on the sabbath, to save life or to destroy it?" After looking around at all of them, he said to him, "Stretch out your hand." He did so, and his hand was restored. But they were filled with fury and discussed with one another what they might do to Jesus. Now during those days he went out to the mountain to pray; and he spent the night in prayer to God.

—LUKE 6:6–12

He said, "Go out and stand on the mountain before the Lord, for the Lord is about to pass by." Now there was a great wind, so strong that it was splitting mountains and breaking rocks in pieces before the Lord, but the Lord was not in the wind; and after the wind an earthquake, but the Lord was not in the earthquake; and after the earthquake a fire, but the Lord was not in the fire; and after the fire a sound of sheer silence.

—1 KINGS 19:11–12

SILENT OBSERVANCES

I stand between the seasons
    winter has retreated—mostly
    spring wakes slowly—reluctantly
        I wait.

A wild goose builds her nest among the reeds
    almost hidden
      revealed only in her movement
        She broods.

A man with a withered hand
    presents a challenge
    to his faith or to You?
      You healed.

Before the waiting, the brooding, or the healing
    came the mountain-splitting wind
    the earthquake and the fire
      Then silence.

Between winter and spring
in building and brooding
through the withered and the healed
after the wind, quake, and flames
the sound of sheer silence remains.

I want to retreat with winter
hide like the goose
cover the withered places
unsure if I can withstand the wind and storms
but
I will awaken with spring
move out of the shadowy reeds
reach for healing
stand still until a new day begins
    to fill me with sacred silence.

MONDAY

He said to his disciples, "Therefore I tell you, do not worry about your life, what you will eat, or about your body, what you will wear. For life is more than food, and the body more than clothing. Consider the ravens: they neither sow nor reap, they have neither storehouse nor barn, and yet God feeds them. Of how much more value are you than the birds! And can any of you by worrying add a single hour to your span of life? If then you are not able to do so small a thing as that, why do you worry about the rest? Consider the lilies, how they grow: they neither toil nor spin; yet I tell you, even Solomon in all his glory was not clothed like one of these. But if God so clothes the grass of the field, which is alive today and tomorrow is thrown into the oven, how much more will he clothe you—you of little faith!

—LUKE 12:22–28

Then the Lord said, "I have observed the misery of my people who are in Egypt; I have heard their cry on account of their taskmasters. Indeed, I know their sufferings, and I have come down to deliver them from the Egyptians, and to bring them up out of that land to a good and broad land, a land flowing with milk and honey . . .

—EXODUS 3:7–8

TOWARD JERUSALEM

The land of milk and honey marks the horizon
    at the edge of my vision
    a few more days of travel

a little more desert sun
a short distance through wilderness
Jerusalem holds such promise
I can see it.

Hear, O Lord, the cries of Your people
        those who live in the shadows
                of poverty and hunger
                homelessness and disease
                war and despair
        those who give voice to worry
        and embody suffering

        and we who hear the cries
                see the needs
                offer nurture, shelter, healing
                wanting peace and hope
        we who speak the prayers of Your people
        witness the injustice.

Deliver us from our taskmasters,
open our eyes to the ravens and lilies.
Remind us all that You know our sufferings
        and will deliver us from misery.

Jerusalem lies just over the next hill,
alive with promise.
Let Your people worry no more . . .

TUESDAY

Praise the Lord! How good it is to sing praises to our God; for he is gracious, and a song of praise is fitting. The Lord builds up Jerusalem; he gathers the outcasts of Israel. He heals the brokenhearted, and binds up their wounds. He determines the number of the stars; he gives to all of them their names. Great is our Lord, and abundant in power; his understanding is beyond measure. The Lord lifts up the downtrodden; he casts the wicked to the ground. Sing to the Lord with thanksgiving; make melody to our God on the lyre. He covers the heavens with clouds, prepares rain for the earth, makes grass grow on the hills. He gives to the animals their food, and to the young ravens when they cry. His delight is not in the strength of the horse, nor his pleasure in the speed of a runner; but the Lord takes pleasure in those who fear him, in those who hope in his steadfast love.

—PSALM 147:1–11

"Come to me, all you that are weary and are carrying heavy burdens, and I will give you rest. Take my yoke upon you, and learn from me; for I am gentle and humble in heart, and you will find rest for your souls. For my yoke is easy, and my burden is light."

—MATTHEW 11:28–30

MY LORD

Broken, beaten child.
Broken, beaten world.
Broken, beaten Crucified One,
    My faith is gone.

But You say:
     Come unto me all who labor
          and are heavy laden
     And I will give you rest.
     Come unto me Thirst and Hunger
     And you shall be no more
     For this is my body broken for you.

Broken, beaten child,
     you bear your wounds in silence.
Broken, beaten world,
     you line the streets with Thirst and Hunger.
Broken, beaten Crucified One,
     I've lost my way.

But You say:
     Come unto me all who labor
          and are heavy laden
     And I will give you rest.
     Come unto me Thirst and Hunger
     And you shall be no more
     For this is my body broken for you.

               Broken, beaten child,
                    I am with you in your silence.
               Broken, beaten world,
                    I weep for love of you.
               I am the Broken, beaten Crucified One,
                    and I call to you:

Come unto me all who labor
　　and are heavy laden
and I will give you rest.
Come unto me Thirst and Hunger
　　and you shall be no more
for this is my body broken for you.

Broken, beaten child,
　　I will bind your broken heart.
Broken, beaten, world,
　　I will raise up the downtrodden.
I am.

And I say:
　　Come unto me all who labor
　　　　and are heavy laden
　　and I will give you rest.
　　Come unto me Thirst and Hunger
　　　　and you shall be no more
　　for this is my body broken for you.

Broken, beaten child
Broken, beaten world
Broken, beaten Crucified One
　　You are my Lord.

　　And I come,
　　　　I come unto you.

WEDNESDAY

Salt is good; but if salt has lost its saltiness, how can you season it? Have salt in yourselves, and be at peace with one another.

—MARK 9:50

Ho, everyone who thirsts, come to the waters; and you that have no money, come, buy and eat! Come, buy wine and milk without money and without price. Why do you spend your money for that which is not bread, and your labor for that which does not satisfy? Listen carefully to me, and eat what is good, and delight yourselves in rich food. Incline your ear, and come to me; listen, so that you may live. I will make with you an everlasting covenant, my steadfast, sure love for David. See, I made him a witness to the peoples, a leader and commander for the peoples. See, you shall call nations that you do not know, and nations that do not know you shall run to you, because of the Lord your God, the Holy One of Israel, for he has glorified you. Seek the Lord while he may be found, call upon him while he is near; let the wicked forsake their way, and the unrighteous their thoughts; let them return to the Lord, that he may have mercy on them, and to our God, for he will abundantly pardon. For my thoughts are not your thoughts, nor are your ways my ways, says the Lord. For as the heavens are higher than the earth, so are my ways higher than your ways and my thoughts than your thoughts. For as the rain and the snow come down from heaven, and do not return there until they have watered the earth, making it bring forth and sprout, giving seed to the sower and bread to the eater, so shall my word be that goes out from my mouth; it shall not return to me empty, but it shall accomplish that which I purpose, and succeed in the thing for which I sent it. For you shall go out in joy, and be led back in peace; the mountains and the hills before you shall burst into song, and all the trees of the field shall clap their hands. Instead of the thorn shall come up the cypress; instead of the brier shall come up the myrtle; and it shall be to the Lord for a memorial, for an everlasting sign that shall not be cut off.

—ISAIAH 55:1–13

TUNE

Lamenting in springtime feels out of tune with the
mountains singing and trees clapping while rivers flow.

I hear the songs of life, unmistakable.
I hear the invitation to the banquet of love.
I hear the promise.

But how do I leave this sorrow
    fresh loss
    old heartbreak
    hunger and thirst unsatisfied
to join the wondrous rhythm of the season?

Let me be still while You are near
    to breathe in the scent of life unfolding
    taste the promise in the salt-laden air
    discover the path that leads to peace.

Soon I will continue on toward Jerusalem.
When I go, I will leave behind
the things that fail to satisfy
    that I may follow You, unburdened, into abundance.

Lamenting in springtime feels out of tune with the
mountains singing and trees clapping while rivers flow.

THURSDAY

And they brought the boy to him. When the spirit saw him, immediately it convulsed the boy, and he fell on the ground and rolled about, foaming at the mouth. Jesus asked the father, "How long has this been happening to him?" And he said, "From childhood. It has often cast him into the fire and into the water, to destroy him; but if you are able to do anything, have pity on us and help us." Jesus said to him, "If you are able!—All things can be done for the one who believes." Immediately the father of the child cried out, "I believe; help my unbelief!" When Jesus saw that a crowd came running together, he rebuked the unclean spirit, saying to it, "You spirit that keeps this boy from speaking and hearing, I command you, come out of him, and never enter him again!" After crying out and convulsing him terribly, it came out, and the boy was like a corpse, so that most of them said, "He is dead." But Jesus took him by the hand and lifted him up, and he was able to stand.

—MARK 9:20–27

When the righteous cry for help, the Lord hears, and rescues them from all their troubles.

—PSALM 34:17

LIFTED UP

No excuse of demons or disease holds me in doubt
even after these weeks of walking with You
knowing that this journey ends soon
I am still uncertain of You
and what You might be able to do.

A father brought his son
just in case what was said about You
held truth.
Could You? Would You? Help a tormented child?
  All that father had to do was believe
    in You
    (or in himself?)

In that moment he recognized his limitations
confessed his belief—and his unbelief
  a moment of honesty so often overlooked
  by most who call on You for help
  in tormenting times.

You honored his faith by lifting up his son
letting him stand on his feet
and walk away from death.

I need to stand and walk . . .

I bring many before You by name
asking You to help
  those who suffer the torment
    of disease and
      relentless, restless spirits.

Sometimes I lack that father's courage
afraid to stand with You
or walk the path of life

But today
with the music of celebration
growing louder with every step,
hear my troubles
    these things that keep me in doubt
    the shadowy silences in my spirit
    and the screaming suffering around me.

Take my hand
let me stand with You.

I believe.
Help my unbelief.

FRIDAY

Then the king will say to those at his right hand, "Come, you that are blessed by my Father, inherit the kingdom prepared for you from the foundation of the world; for I was hungry and you gave me food, I was thirsty and you gave me something to drink, I was a stranger and you welcomed me, I was naked and you gave me clothing, I was sick and you took care of me, I was in prison and you visited me." Then the righteous will answer him, "Lord, when was it that we saw you hungry and gave you food, or thirsty and gave you something to drink? And when was it that we saw you a stranger and welcomed you, or naked and gave you clothing? And when was it that we saw you sick or in prison and visited you?" And the king will answer them, "Truly I tell you, just as you did it to one of the least of these who are members of my family, you did it to me."

—MATTHEW 25:34–40

The spirit of the Lord God is upon me, because the Lord has anointed me; he has sent me to bring good news to the oppressed, to bind up the brokenhearted, to proclaim liberty to the captives, and release to the prisoners . . .

—ISAIAH 61:1

A REMINDER

Oppression
Heartbreak
Captivity
Imprisonment
When will we learn?

How many lives must be lost
to the demons of today
before we see You
in those we discard and dismiss
as we comfort only ourselves?

Open our eyes before it is too late
for the hungry and thirsty
the stranger and the naked
the sick and the imprisoned
in us and among us.

Remind us of all we stand to lose
when we close our eyes
ignore the devastation around us
distance ourselves from need
and turn from following You.

Fill us with Your will to step
into life today to bring good news
of liberty and release
to those who live brokenhearted
cast out and not seen.

SATURDAY

This is my commandment, that you love one another as I have loved you. No one has greater love than this, to lay down one's life for one's friends. You are my friends if you do what I command you. I do not call you servants any longer, because the servant does not know what the master is doing; but I have called you friends, because I have made known to you everything that I have heard from my Father. You did not choose me but I chose you. And I appointed you to go and bear fruit, fruit that will last . . .

—JOHN 15:12:16A

You shall love the Lord your God with all your heart, with all your soul, and with all your might.

—DEUTERONOMY 6:5

A CHOICE

Sounds of celebration float on the air
and I want to turn away
from the faces and voices of need
that will cry and call out
as the mood of the city shifts
in the days to come.

You spoke simple words to Your disciples
long ago
a command to love as You love
without hesitation, without condition.

All the faces in the crowd
who will sing for joy
cry out in anger
weep in despair
belong to You . . .

I am reluctant to leave this wilderness
of my being
to walk with You through
all that is to come
knowing Your command to love as You love.

Remind me of all the places we have walked
my darkness and Your light
my despair and Your hope
my doubt and Your love
just to arrive at this place
where past and present meet
and You ask me to love for Your sake.

If You have chosen me as Your friend
then I must be ready to go with You
into this city of fickle crowds
to share in all that is to come
without hesitation or condition.
As You have loved,
may I go and do likewise . . .

7

From Celebration to Suffering

I will not leave you orphaned; I am coming to you. In a little while the world will no longer see me, but you will see me; because I live, you also will live.

—JOHN 14:18–19

PALM SUNDAY

When they were approaching Jerusalem, at Bethphage and Bethany, near the Mount of Olives, he sent two of his disciples and said to them, "Go into the village ahead of you, and immediately as you enter it, you will find tied there a colt that has never been ridden; untie it and bring it. If anyone says to you, 'Why are you doing this?' just say this, 'The Lord needs it and will send it back here immediately.'" They went away and found a colt tied near a door, outside in the street. As they were untying it, some of the bystanders said to them, "What are you doing, untying the colt?" They told them what Jesus had said; and they allowed them to take it. Then they brought the colt to Jesus and threw their cloaks on it; and he sat on it. Many people spread their cloaks on the road, and others spread leafy branches that they had cut in the fields. Then those who went ahead and those who followed were shouting, "Hosanna! Blessed is the one who comes in the name of the Lord! Blessed is the coming kingdom of our ancestor David! Hosanna in the highest heaven!" Then he entered Jerusalem and went into the temple; and when he had looked around at everything, as it was already late, he went out to Bethany with the twelve.

—MARK 11:1–11

Rejoice greatly, O daughter Zion! Shout aloud, O daughter Jerusalem! Lo, your king comes to you; triumphant and victorious is he, humble and riding on a donkey, on a colt, the foal of a donkey.

—ZECHARIAH 9:9

PALM SUNDAY

Two parades cross town
giving onlookers a simple choice
   between Pontius Pilate
   and Jesus of Nazareth—
     between power
     and humility.

   One rides into town
   on a big white horse
   with shouts of acclamation
   and a full Roman guard—
     breast plates shining,
     spears gripped, at the ready (no offense)—
     securing peace.
Who would not be tempted?

   The Other rides quietly
   on a young donkey
   with little fanfare
   and a few lowly disciples—
     dusty clothes and dirty feet,
     hands empty, accepting all (without defense)—
     questioning security.
   Where is the temptation here?

   Roman rule is safe and sure
     no risk
     no change
     no choice.

Jesus' way breaks rules
risks everything
   changes everything
   challenges everything.

If I choose the big, fancy parade
   just for today
will it shift the course of this week?
   Not likely.

Jesus will ride to the temple if I am not looking
and turn toward Bethany with his friends.
He will gather for Passover in an upper room
   wash feet
   break bread
   sing hymns
   go to a garden to pray.

If I turn to Rome even for a moment
Jesus' disciples will still fall asleep
   leave him alone
      until the soldiers come
      and Judas betrays him with a kiss
      and Peter follows his impulses . . .

If I fall for the glamour
Jesus will still be arrested
   found guilty without trial
   Pontius Pilate will wash his hands
      (as if he could cleanse his own sins)
   the whip will crack and blood will flow
   the innocent condemned.

What difference will it make if I am not there
　just this once?
　　No one will notice if I turn away
　　　from the humble man who rides
　　　with his toes dragging in the sand.

I do not need to see prophecy fulfilled
with branches and cloaks
tossed to the ground—
a poor pavement for the Son of God.

Will it matter if I don't wonder
why he rides up and looks at the Temple
　before heading off in another direction?
If I step away from the crowd before
　brokenness and betrayal,
　　darkness and denial,
　　　will any difference be made?

If I am not there today,
I don't have to hear the cries for crucifixion
or see the tears of anguish in his mother's eyes
later.

One day, one parade, one person

One less Hosanna
　One less cloak on the ground
　　One less face in the crowd.

On the other side of town,
   cheers and shouts
   instruments and song
   proclaim power and presence.
      The white horse and the Centurion stir up dust
      and put on a show.
      Echoes fade fast and the crowd stands lifeless,
      waiting for more
      in the oppressive heat.

Who would know if I went there?
One more to wave and sing
   covered in dust
   awed by power
   blinded by the glare of empty promises,
   marked by the shadows of Roman spears.
      One more face in the crowd.

If I avoid the triumph of today,
   the quiet cleansing of Thursday
      the deep silence giving way to deeper darkness
         in the garden and on the cross,
If I do not witness
   the fickle crowd shouting "Save Us!" today
   and "Crucify him!" tomorrow
      the hope cracking wide open
      into abysmal despair,

What else will I miss?
  Rome changes nothing with its finery;
  it always rules in falsity and illusion
  securing obedience with fear
  and peace with force.

Jesus rides through the city
  asking for nothing
  but for us to have courage
  to bear witness
    all the way through to the early morning
    on the first day of the week
    so our eyes will be opened
    again.

Ride on!
Take me with you (feet dragging and all) . . .

MONDAY

Then one of the twelve, who was called Judas Iscariot, went to the chief priests and said, "What will you give me if I betray him to you?" They paid him thirty pieces of silver. And from that moment he began to look for an opportunity to betray him.

—MATTHEW 26:14–16

"Whenever you stand praying, forgive, if you have anything against anyone; so that your Father in heaven may also forgive you your trespasses."

—MARK 11:25

FOR THE LOVE OF JUDAS

Judas must have walked in the shadows
to lose sight of You—
    even for a moment.
Perhaps he felt slighted
    or jealous of one of the others
    or maybe he felt that You
    had forgotten him.
It could have been anger or impulse or
something else entirely
but he traded You for thirty pieces of silver
    and he did not bargain for
    losing himself in the deal.

He never recovered from his act of betrayal.
If he knew of Your forgiveness
he could not forgive himself.

How many have betrayed You
for less than silver
   and paid the same price of a life lost
   in trying to earn forgiveness
   already offered?

I have walked into darkness
away from You more times than I can count
unable to believe You call me by name
and claim me as Yours.

Even now, I stand in awe of You.
You let Judas be Judas
knowing how it would go
   and what it would cost him
   and the price You would pay.

If You loved Judas enough to let
him make his mistake,
so You must love all of us
who stumble in our efforts
to follow You
even when we choose to turn away.

TUESDAY

Jesus said to them, "The light is with you for a little longer. Walk while you have the light, so that the darkness may not overtake you. If you walk in the darkness, you do not know where you are going. While you have the light, believe in the light, so that you may become children of light."

—JOHN 12:35–36

In God, whose word I praise, in the Lord, whose word I praise, in God I trust; I am not afraid. What can a mere mortal do to me? My vows to you I must perform, O God; I will render thank offerings to you. For you have delivered my soul from death, and my feet from falling, so that I may walk before God in the light of life.

—PSALM 56:10–13

THANK OFFERINGS

Echoes of hosannas fade
as the forgotten palm branches dry
to be remembered another year.
The excitement and promise of
pageantry and parade
cannot long withstand the noise
of today.

Distracting demands of daily living
take my focus from You
no matter what I vow.

I promise to walk with You
in the light
with my offerings of grateful thanks,
but the darkness is misleading.

Thoughts of war and poverty,
homelessness and hopelessness,
the confused and the forgotten,
victims and sufferers
follow me, call out for my attention.
You have blessed me with much—
should I not do more?

And more and more?
until I am spinning in the dark,
light forgotten,
nearly lost myself
again.
You have not
ever lost sight of me.

Even now, when I stand still,
quiet, listening
in the sounds of sheer silence
I hear You.
In the deepest of my dark
when I turn to You
Your light shines.

In my hand is a single palm leaf
to remind me that You passed this way
and You want me to follow
no matter what other voices
call to me, making me forget
that salvation is Yours to give;
I can offer hope and light
if I am paying attention.

Mostly, You want me to remember
to seek after Your ways—
unafraid—
to reach out with Your hands
or speak with Your words
or walk in Your light . . .

When I stand in the stillness of You
I can sing "Hosanna!" right out loud.
This is my thankful offering.

WEDNESDAY

Then they came to Jerusalem. And he entered the temple and began to drive out those who were selling and those who were buying in the temple, and he overturned the tables of the money changers and the seats of those who sold doves; and he would not allow anyone to carry anything through the temple. He was teaching and saying, "Is it not written, 'My house shall be called a house of prayer for all the nations'? But you have made it a den of robbers."

—MARK 11:15–17

CHANGING TODAY

I cannot help but wonder
what You would do to the church
today?

You came and broke all the rules—
welcoming the outcast
cleansing the unclean
healing the sick
   even on the Sabbath

You challenged the keepers of the Law
to find a better way—
a way of life, of love, of hope—
that honored You.

We may not change money at our doors
or sell doves to those who enter
but we keep our own laws
and exclude any number of
    outcasts
    unclean
    sick
      even on the Sabbath.

You spoke of love and peace.
How did we turn this into ways of division and
hatred?
You warned about worshipping Tradition
in place of You.

Mostly, we don't think about it
though sometimes
when we are confronted with someone
wholly different,
we want to turn away
or close the door
or bar them from Your house,
Your table,
our presence.

It is so easy for us to condemn those
early Temple money changers
for corrupting the House of God
until we pause . . .
Surely we are not the people You
would want us to be.

Tired, reluctant worshippers
who fail to call you "Friend."
Sing Your praises now and then,
maybe.
But talk with You,
walk with You,
keep watch
and wait with You?
Not often enough and so very seldom
in the houses we call Yours
    even on the Sabbath.

We are too busy closing our doors,
making our rules,
doing what has always been done
to notice that we have long since
forgotten You.

You won't find money changers
or dove sellers
today
but perhaps You ought to come
and turn us all out on the streets
until we realize
that all are welcome
in Your house
at Your table
    even on the Sabbath.

MAUNDY THURSDAY

"I have said these things to you while I am still with you. But the Advocate, the Holy Spirit, whom the Father will send in my name, will teach you everything, and remind you of all that I have said to you. Peace I leave with you; my peace I give to you. I do not give to you as the world gives. Do not let your hearts be troubled, and do not let them be afraid.

—JOHN 14:25–27

He was despised and rejected by others; a man of suffering and acquainted with infirmity; and as one from whom others hide their faces he was despised, and we held him of no account.

—ISAIAH 53:3

BETRAYAL

foot washing
the body broken
the cup poured out
promises of peace
betrayal

prayer in a garden
keeping watch
falling asleep
anguish
a simple kiss
betrayal

a trial
a mockery
condemnation
denial
betrayal

> You washed their feet
> to remind them to serve one another
> You offered bread and wine
> in a covenant of forgiveness
> You spoke peace to stem
> the tide of fear that was coming
> You knew how it would go
>
> after the song You went to pray
> asking them to keep watch
> but they could not stay awake
> with You or for You
> leaving You alone
> until Judas came with his kiss
> surprising all but You
>
> from high priest to Roman official
> a judgment left to the mindless crowd
> determined Your death
> while the disciples scattered
> with fear in their hearts and denial on their lips
> abandoning You once more

Today we remember and try to serve
one another
gathering at Your table
with broken bread and wine poured out
in a covenant intended for all
seeking forgiveness
hoping for peace
in the eternal flow of fear
we need to find You here

we sing and pray
wanting to keep watch
with You and for You
wishing that betrayal would not come
and the kiss will not be ours
You will not be surprised

it is not for judgment and death
that we abandon You
though we are still swayed by the noise of the crowd
influenced by mindless fear and ready denial
no matter how hard we try
we, too, will scatter—afraid
before the night is over

betrayal

GOOD FRIDAY

When it was noon, darkness came over the whole land until three in the afternoon. At three o'clock Jesus cried out with a loud voice, "Eloi, Eloi, lema sabachthani?" which means, "My God, my God, why have you forsaken me?" When some of the bystanders heard it, they said, "Listen, he is calling for Elijah." And someone ran, filled a sponge with sour wine, put it on a stick, and gave it to him to drink, saying, "Wait, let us see whether Elijah will come to take him down." Then Jesus gave a loud cry and breathed his last. And the curtain of the temple was torn in two, from top to bottom. Now when the centurion, who stood facing him, saw that in this way he breathed his last, he said, "Truly this man was God's Son!" There were also women looking on from a distance; among them were Mary Magdalene, and Mary the mother of James the younger and of Joses, and Salome. These used to follow him and provided for him when he was in Galilee; and there were many other women who had come up with him to Jerusalem.

—MARK 15:33–41

Surely he has borne our infirmities and carried our diseases; yet we accounted him stricken, struck down by God, and afflicted. But he was wounded for our transgressions, crushed for our iniquities; upon him was the punishment that made us whole, and by his bruises we are healed. All we like sheep have gone astray; we have all turned to our own way, and the Lord has laid on him the iniquity of us all

—ISAIAH 53:4–6

GOOD FRIDAY

darkness clouded the earth
while You hung on a cross
even with the power of life
hanging before their eyes,
the crowd failed to notice
You

healed the sick
gave sight to the blind
opened the ears of the deaf
fed the hungry
touched the outcast
raised the dead

and it was not enough
or was it too much

in that moment before death
You were forsaken
as no one has ever been
before or since
You died to bring us into
relationship with God
unknowable until You
walked among us
and offered Your life for ours

some offered only scorn
even then
oblivious to the dark skies
and prophecies fulfilled

at Your last breath
the temple curtain tore
in two—top to bottom
and a centurion recognized
You

as the faithful women watched from a distance
the disciples from hidden doorways
places shadowy with fear
and anguish
while others simply watched
in fascinated horror

no matter who bore witness that day
or who averted their eyes
in pain or shame or fear or grief
no one saw the change in life
and death that happened in those
pre-Sabbath hours
of darkness

who could have foreseen
the curtain torn down to
nothing veiling God
from humanity?

we still seldom notice
the darkened skies
the curtain torn
the scriptures fulfilled
we question what happened that day
as we hide in our doubts about
You

who gave Your life so that we
could live fully
we can hardly hold this possibility
as we stand at the foot of the cross
today
reluctant to let go of the sins
You took with You
long ago

as You suffered death
and changed the world
forever

so why do we cling to our unworthiness
unable to see that You made us worth
Your life and death?
we continue to separate ourselves
from You again and again
lost in our sins
failing to notice we have been forgiven

HOLY SATURDAY

Then they arrived at the country of the Gerasenes, which is opposite Galilee. As he stepped out on land, a man of the city who had demons met him. For a long time he had worn no clothes, and he did not live in a house but in the tombs. When he saw Jesus, he fell down before him and shouted at the top of his voice, "What have you to do with me, Jesus, Son of the Most High God? I beg you, do not torment me"—for Jesus had commanded the unclean spirit to come out of the man. (For many times it had seized him; he was kept under guard and bound with chains and shackles, but he would break the bonds and be driven by the demon into the wilds.) Jesus then asked him, "What is your name?" He said, "Legion"; for many demons had entered him. They begged him not to order them to go back into the abyss. Now there on the hillside a large herd of swine was feeding; and the demons begged Jesus to let them enter these. So he gave them permission. Then the demons came out of the man and entered the swine, and the herd rushed down the steep bank into the lake and was drowned. When the swineherds saw what had happened, they ran off and told it in the city and in the country. Then people came out to see what had happened, and when they came to Jesus, they found the man from whom the demons had gone sitting at the feet of Jesus, clothed and in his right mind. And they were afraid. Those who had seen it told them how the one who had been possessed by demons had been healed. Then all the people of the surrounding country of the Gerasenes asked Jesus to leave them; for they were seized with great fear. So he got into the boat and returned. The man from whom the demons had gone begged that he might be with him; but Jesus sent him away, saying, "Return to your home, and declare how much God has done for you." So he went away, proclaiming throughout the city how much Jesus had done for him.

—LUKE 8:26–39

I was ready to be sought out by those who did not ask, to be found by those who did not seek me. I said, "Here I am, here I am," to a nation that did not call on my name.

—ISAIAH 65:1

ONE AMONG MANY

You stepped out of a boatful
   of doubt
to face a man who had none.
Naked, in a wild place,
   out of his right mind,
     he knew You.

Legion changed nothing
   except the direction of swine,
   even then, only with Your permission.

A man who came to sit at Your feet
   in freedom and wholeness
   inspired fear enough to drive
     You away
       leaving one man to speak
       Your name.

Legion lives today
   nearly always welcomed by those
   clothed in righteousness
   and assured of right-mindedness.

We who choose not to see

those cast out—
    barely alive in the tombs
    of our ignorance—
We mistake the lost ones for swine
unable to see humanity
    in those who rock our boats.
    They call your name—
    rightly—
    while we huddle in fear.

Those who hide at the edges of life
    are numerous
But we who turn away
    with Your name on our lips . . .

We are legion.

Cast us into a mind right
    enough to sit with You—
        in the tombs
        in the wild places
        among the lost—
            naked or clothed.
            Free of fear.
            Wholly one . . .
                Legion no more.

EASTER

When the sabbath was over, Mary Magdalene, and Mary the mother of James, and Salome bought spices, so that they might go and anoint him. And very early on the first day of the week, when the sun had risen, they went to the tomb. They had been saying to one another, "Who will roll away the stone for us from the entrance to the tomb?" When they looked up, they saw that the stone, which was very large, had already been rolled back. As they entered the tomb, they saw a young man, dressed in a white robe, sitting on the right side; and they were alarmed. But he said to them, "Do not be alarmed; you are looking for Jesus of Nazareth, who was crucified. He has been raised; he is not here. Look, there is the place they laid him. But go, tell his disciples and Peter that he is going ahead of you to Galilee; there you will see him, just as he told you." So they went out and fled from the tomb, for terror and amazement had seized them; and they said nothing to anyone, for they were afraid.

—MARK 16:1–8

You have turned my mourning into dancing; you have taken off my sackcloth and clothed me with joy, so that my soul may praise you and not be silent. O Lord my God, I will give thanks to you forever.

—PSALM 30:11–12

MOURNING INTO DANCING

three women, and maybe more, went to anoint You
early in the morning after two nights of grieving
with only the hope of giving you a proper burial
to move them beyond their tears

their expectations underestimated You
as an angel greeted them in Your otherwise
empty tomb

terror and amazement warred within them
as well they should—
who could face resurrection without
a healthy dose of fear
widened with amazement?

initially the women fled (who would have stayed?)
but they later told their story to Peter and others
so often repeated over the centuries
we have lost our terror
and most of our amazement

death defeated somehow becomes ambiguous
inspiring little more than ambivalence

on this Easter Day, fill our hearts
with amazement and terror
that we might feel the extraordinary
possibility of new life
right here
where we stand

let us flee with the women
as we realize what you have done
for us
and then let us proclaim
that You are risen
as amazement
reshapes our terror
and sets us free to dance with joy

Scripture Index

OLD TESTAMENT

Luke

John